IMAGES
of Ireland

BANBRIDGE

Members of the Smyth family of Smyth's Weaving Company, Brookfield, Banbridge preparing to go for a drive in their Irish Jaunting Car, outside Brookfield House, *c.* 1910.

IMAGES
of Ireland

BANBRIDGE

Compiled by
Angela Dillon

First published 1997
Copyright © Banbridge & District Historical Society, 1997

Gill and Macmillan Publishers
Goldenbridge, Inchicore
Dublin 8

ISBN 0 7171 2643 9

Typesetting and origination by
The Chalford Publishing Company
Printed in Great Britain by
Bailey Print, Dursley, Gloucestershire

Also published in the *Images of Ireland* series:
East Belfast (Keith Haines)

Downshire Bridge and The Cut, Banbridge, *c.* 1910.

Contents

Introduction

Banbridge is situated in the townland of Ballyvalley which translated from the Irish language means 'the townland of the road'. The road referred to came into the town over Ballymoney Hill and crossed the River Bann at a shallow ford near the present bridge in the town. Banbridge lies approximately 14 miles north-east of Newry and 24 miles south-east of Belfast and forms part of the parish of Seapatrick in the Barony of Upper Iveagh. This land was once the property of the Magennis family from whom it was purchased in 1615 by Sir Marmaduke Whitechurch, whose descendants, the Hills (Downshire Family of Hillsborough) and the Whytes of Loughbrickland, inherited the lands on which the town of Banbridge is situated. Banbridge is first mentioned as a town in 1712 when a bridge was erected over the River Bann. The new mail-coach road then diverged from the old road, which had crossed the river at Ballykeel Ford in Huntly Glen, to cross at the new bridge. The town was situated on the side of a hill overlooking the picturesque Bann Valley and was surrounded by good farmland. It commanded breathtaking views of the countryside all around. In the early days the town consisted of a tiny cluster of houses around the new bridge. Bridge Street and Newry Street were the principal streets, the former being situated on a very steep hill on top of which stood an attractive market house. The ground floor of the Market House consisted of open arched areas suitable for the sale of farm produce and linen, while the first floor was used for public meetings.

The old inn, The Bunch of Grapes, stood to the right of the Market House. On the east gable wall was the legend 'Accommodation for Man and Beast', and it was said of this old inn that it was famous for good cheer. The weary traveller was assured of a good meal and comfortable sleeping quarters; the old-fashioned fireplaces were wide, with roaring peat fires, and hanging from hooks above was a plentiful supply of hams and dried beef. In a corner against the wall stood a large meal chest that was filled with oatmeal for making oatcakes and stirabout (porridge). The top storey housed the bedrooms and sitting room, which was used as a meeting place for the local Masonic lodge for many years.

At one time a 'Court of Pie Pondre' was in existence for the settlement of disputes at fairs and markets of which it is stated that, 'Justice was done as speedily as dust could fall from the foot'. This was one of the most ancient tribunals known in English Common Law.

The old road from Belfast to Dublin came over Ballymoney Hill, down Hill Street, over the bridge into Bridge Street, up the great hill into Newry Street and up the old road to Loughbrickland, now known as Fort Street. The present Newry Road was not made until 1819. In 1733 power was granted by parliament to erect turnpikes and take tolls. The old turnpike house at the Fort Street end of Newry Road was erected as a dwelling for the toll-keeper who collected the money from those wishing to travel the road to Newry. Access was by a large gate across the road at this point. The old turnpike cottage was demolished some time in the 1960s to make way for road-widening at Fort Street.

The first post office was opened in Banbridge in 1784. Prior to this Banbridge was served by the neighbouring village of Loughbrickland which had had a post office since 1670 when mail was carried by mounted post boys riding alone. This practice continued until mail-coaches were established in 1788-89 when passengers were protected by a guard, armed with a blunderbuss, mounted behind.

The Downshire Arms Hotel was built as a posting inn in 1816. Here the mail-coaches would stop to change horses and let the weary travellers have a rest and refreshments. A post-horn would signal time for departure on the next stage of the journey to Dublin. The old inn still stands in Newry Street and is little changed since those far-off days.

By the late 1880s the town was beginning to take shape with the erection of many fine buildings, which have added greatly to the appearance of Banbridge, giving it an air of distinction and elegance all of its own. Many changes have taken place over the years, which have further enhanced and benefited the town as a whole, making it a pleasant and friendly place to live in. The days of the family grocer have gone and large supermarkets have taken their place. The old streets with their two-up-two-down houses where doors were always open and neighbour helped neighbour, have also been replaced by large housing estates. However, no longer do people have to carry water from the pump in the street and boil water for washing clothes or use dry toilets at the bottom of the yard. Now people can have a better lifestyle and take their families on holidays and children are better educated and can look forward to better jobs and wages. Banbridge is now more of a middle-class town. With the linen industry virtually gone, it has become a dormitory town with people living here but working elsewhere, a far cry from its early beginnings in 1712.

The breezes blow o'er lake and wold,
And happy homes afar,
But memory wakes the days of old,
That saw my natal star.
A wider world my spirit fills,
But partial eyes would scan,
The dear surrounding scented hills,
That shade the flowing Bann.

(from *Echoes of the Bann* by John McKibben)

One
Around Banbridge

Bridge Street, Banbridge, *c.* 1900.

Master James McClean of Gospel Lane School, Banbridge, *c.* 1932. Gospel Lane School was at the bottom of Rathfriland Street. Master McClean was well-thought-of by the children and was indeed a good teacher. He lived at Riversley House in Church Street.

Old Police Station, Banbridge, *c.* 1921. This was before Ireland was partitioned, and the police force was then known as the Royal Irish Constabulary (RIC). The station was originally built in 1860 for the RIC and as the Marquis of Downshire's Estate office. It was used by the RUC until a new station was built across the street in the 1990s.

A group of RUC constables outside Banbridge Old Police Station in the 1930s or '40s.

Mr Sam Gilmore owned a garage in Bridge Street and is pictured here with his two daughters and son, *c.* 1920.

Advertisement for Gilmore's garage from the *Banbridge Household Almanac* of 1926.

Unknown gentleman and dog in veteran car at Iveagh House, one of the homes of the Ferguson family, on the Castlewellan Road, Banbridge, c. 1907.

Mr Fleming of Bridge Street, Banbridge with his penny-farthing bicycle around the turn of the century.

Pupils and staff of Banbridge Academy in 1928 when the school shared the Old Technical Building in Downshire Road. Originally built as the Carnegie Library and Technical School in 1902, the building was extended in 1910 (when the Ferguson annexe was erected by Mr N.D. and Mr T.S. Ferguson in memory of their parents) and again in 1927. In 1947 Banbridge

McMurray and Co.'s shop in Bridge Street, which was demolished in August 1997 owing to structural faults. This old family firm has been run by McMurrays for the past 77 years. The shop will be rebuilt in the same style at a future date.

Academy purchased Edenderry House from the Ferguson family and over the years it has been developed and extended into a fine school while still retaining the beautiful façade of Edenderry House as its centrepiece.

Mrs Agnes Bell of Burn Hill, Newry Street, with her young family in 1915. From left: Jenny, Maisie, Margaret, Agnes, Joseph and Barbara. Inset is a photograph of her husband, Joseph Bell, who was killed at Gallipoli in August 1915.

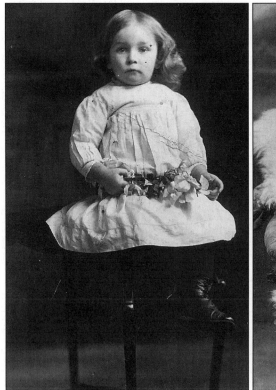

Barbara Bell (*left*), aged 4, in 1918. Maisie Bell, aged 2, in 1915 (*right*).

Mr and Mrs James Pearson of Burn Hill, Newry Street, 1910.

Mr and Mrs William Flanagan and daughters of Newry Street, 1919.

The wedding of Mr Joseph Burns and Miss Maisie Bell on 23 December 1931. Matron of honour was Mrs Margaret Wells and best man was James Wells.

Unknown Banbridge soldier of the First World War (1914-18).

Left: Mr Joseph Burns of Kenlis Street, Banbridge, who was a lance bombardier with the 4th Searchlight Battalion Royal Artillery, *c.* 1940. *Right*: Miss Molly Flanagan (later Mrs T. Wilson) in her WAAF uniform, *c.* 1940.

Left: Paul Burns as a sprightly five-year-old in 1946. *Right*: Miss Pat Wilson in the sixty-year-old Bell family christening robe in 1949.

'C' Company, 5th Battalion, Royal Irish Fusiliers (TA) pictured at Ballyedmund Camp in June 1949. From left, back row: T. Maginnes, R. Clydesdale, D. McMullan, R. McDowell, J. Shannon, S. Boyle, D. Cochrane, E. Stewart, J. McFadden, P. Devlin, W. Gracey, W. Porterfield; third row: W. Nimick, G. McFadden, E. Herron, T. McDowell, R. Spratt, W. Gibson, F. Manson, W. Clydesdale, V. Harries, H. Giffen, F. Baxter, J. Hughes; second row: R. Woods, W. Gracey, N. Kinnin, C. Campbell, H. Scott, M. Small, T. Molloy, R. Baker, J. McPolin, W. Pollock, T. Wilson, P. Davidson, J. Anderson; front row: A. Hilland, F. Harper, R. Foster, C. Meldrum, T. Hawthorne, A. Allen, W. Hobden, J. Keenan, J. Clowney, E. Armstrong, S. McClune.

Three unknown lads from the Yorkshire and Lancashire Regiment who were stationed at Chinauley House, Banbridge during the Second World War. This regiment was known locally as the 'Y and L's' or 'Young and Lovelies'.

Banbridge Home Guard in 1940 making use of one of the lorries belonging to Anthony Cowdy & Sons Ltd, one of the local linen bleaching and finishing companies which utilised the water of the River Bann and kept Banbridge at the forefront of linen production.

'A' Company, 4th Down Battalion, Ulster Home Guard marching through The Cut at their standing-down parade at the end of the Second World War.

'A' Company, 4th Down Battalion, Ulster Home Guard on the Newry Road beside the old Baptist church in February 1941.

Advertisement from c. 1952.

The colour party preparing for inspection by Lord Edward Carson during the Ulster Volunteer Force rally at Lenaderg in 1912.

Ulster Volunteer Force nurses, who later manned a military hospital at Dunbarton House, Gilford, during the First World War, awaiting inspection at the Lenaderg rally in 1912.

Ulster Volunteer Force members lined up for inspection by Lord Edward Carson at Lenaderg in 1912 during the Home Rule Crisis.

The Young family who were drapers at 'The Arcade' in Bridge Street, Banbridge for many years, pictured *c*. 1916. The young gentleman on the extreme left is Mr Joseph Young, the last member of the family to manage the shop and also a town councillor for many years. The other two gentlemen at the back served in the First World War.

The Bann Bridge and the bottom of Bridge Street from the River Bann during a river-straightening scheme in the 1960s. The building on the left, which belonged to the Simms family, eventually began to sink into the river and was demolished in the early 1990s. The third building along was 'The Arcade' where the Young family carried on their drapery business.

Joseph Burns and John Hanna outside Banbridge British Legion Hall on Remembrance Day, 1963.

Bob Anderson on washboard and Paul Burns on guitar in Newcastle, July 1958.

The Starlight Serenaders, *c.* 1948. Ennis Boyd (piano), Alex Martin (accordion), Gerry Crothers (drums and vocals), Brian Neeson (sax and clarinet), Joe McClory (double bass).

Anderson's Rhythm Band, 1948. Amongst those pictured are Mrs J.R. Bambrick, Bertie Magill, James Anderson and Herbert Anderson.

A well-known gentleman in days gone by in Banbridge was Billy Moohan. Billy, better known as the fiddler, carried his faithful instrument everywhere with him and would freely oblige people with a tune. He was also a regular at hockey matches in the town.

Elizabeth Belshaw, otherwise known as 'Din', was another well-known character around Banbridge.

Banbridge Chamber of Commerce dinner, 1970s.

Group outside Donacloney Presbyterian Church, near Banbridge, after rededication of the rebuilt church in 1900.

At play in Banbridge in times gone by. This group of children were gathered outside Jardine's sweet shop in Reilly Street in the mid-1950s. The owners of the shop were Joe and Anne Jardine and the children in the picture are Jeffrey Whiteside, twins Ian and Yvonne Brown, Laureen Revell, -?-.

Employees from Ballydown Works, pictured in the summer of 1953. Amongst those included are Margaret McChesney, Joan McGivern, Angela Sands, Josie Sloane and Lily Devlin.

Seapatrick Parish Junior Bible class on an outing to Newcastle Co. Down, 1940s.

First Banbridge Wolf Cub Pack (Bannside) pictured on the Castlewellan Road in the mid-1950s. Leaders at the back were Miss Muriel Davidson and Miss Edna Beck. Also pictured are, back row: David Robb, Kenneth Witherow, Melvyn Brown, Christopher Moore, Drew Hudson, Douglas Stevenson; middle row: Laurence Williams, Wynford Jackson, Ronald Jones, Eric Witherow, John Weir, Jack Arlow, Desmond Ervine, Jim Arlow, Trevor Todd; front row: Robin Ervine, Colin Cromie, Nigel Chambers, Colin Weir, Stanley Harkness, Jim Robinson, Cyril Poots.

Seapatrick parish church choir standing in front of the East Window which depicts da Vinci's *Last Supper*, c. 1990.

Scarva Street Presbyterian Church choir pictured after Harvest Thanksgiving in 1995.

Visit of Jack Doyle and Tom Prewett, two storytellers from South Carolina, c. 1994. From left, front row: Doreen McBride, Tom Prewett, Angela Dillon, J. Doyle and Billy Ritchie; back row: -?-, R. Moles, -?-, E. Moles, A. McQuaid, J. Napier, M. McClimond, -?-, -?-.

Banbridge Golf Club Lady President's Day winners, 1997. From left, back row: Aileen McVey, Freda Richardson, Kathy Ward and Maeve Fee; front row: Mildred Hodgett, Rosemary Cocks (Lady President) and Phylis McElherron.

Banbridge Historical Society committee, 1986. From left: Helen Adams, Noel Bloomer, Jack Hamilton, Frank Downey and Gordon Lyle.

Some of the Banbridge Historical Society members, led by their chairman Norman Kerr, who took part in a ramble along the Banbridge to Scarva railway line in June 1997.

Historical Society members on their way to the Public Records Office in 1996.

Historical Society members on a visit to the new High School in 1996.

A group of children from Church Street School in the 1920s.

Pupils at Church Street School, 1956.

This picture, taken at the old Church School on an evening in the 1920s shows the famous 2nd Banbridge Scout and Guide Pierrot Troop, who used their time and talents in aid of charity.

The cast from *My Fair Lady*, produced by Ballydown Primary School in 1997.

Pupils from Meenan Old School, Loughbrickland, 1924.

Pupils from Loughbrickland No 2 School in 1925.

More pupils from Loughbrickland No 2 School in 1925.

Loughbrickland Controlled Primary school
1979/80

Pupils from Loughbrickland Controlled Primary School, 1979-80.

Pupils from Friars Place Public Elementary School in 1926.

Pupils from Friars Place Public Elementary School in 1928.

More pupils from Friars Place Public Elementary School in 1928 with teachers S.J. Johnston and Miss E. Mercer.

Mr E.F. Smyth and partner in his early Renault, outside Brookfield House in 1912.

Mr John Mercer (*left*) on his penny-farthing bicycle in 1997. *Right*: advertisement for J.H. Blackburn, agent for Renault cars, from the *Banbridge Household Almanac*, 1928.

Mr Gilbert Beck beside his horse-drawn bread-cart in the 1920s.

Mr and Mrs Gilbert Beck with their children, Emma, Joe, Gilbert, and William, outside their home at Cascum in the late 1920s.

A group of linen workers from Smyth's Weaving Company in the early 1900s.

A group of linen workers from the Banbridge area, *c.* 1932.

Members of staff of Walkers Factory (later Robinson and Cleavers) in 1927. From left: Mr McKeown, Mr A. Bunting, Mr H. Bunting, Mr J. McKinstry, -?-, Miss M. Greenfield, Mr W.J. Greenfield, Mr Hanlon and Mr B. Tweedy.

Inside the winding department at Wm. Walker & Co. Ltd in 1939.

Winding department staff at Wm. Walker & Co. Ltd in 1939. From left, back row: Minnie Roney, May Dale, Mrs Redpath, Anne Morrow, Rita Clyde, Mrs Magill, Gladys Irvine, Mrs Derby, Clara Pilson, Dorothy Baker, Doris Lyle; second row: Ella Strain, Mrs Cairns, Esther Dale, Mrs Currie, Mrs Lutton, Bella Lutton, Annie Moore, Dolly Baird, Mrs Mallon, Sarah Jardine, Jim McMaster; third row: Maureen Magee, Jean Best, May Best, Mrs Graham, Carrie Ross, Mr Rogers, Nellie Mackin, Mary McMaster, Mrs Willis, Mrs Campbell, Tessie Murphy; fourth row: May Cochrane, Lilia Baird, Violet Beck, Madge Graham, Georgie Campbell, Edna Ervine, Mrs Barr.

The mechanical department at Dunbar McMaster & Co. Ltd of Gilford in 1937.

Nos 4 and 5 Preparation Departments at Dunbar McMaster & Co. Ltd of Gilford, 1937.

Norman Kerr, chairman of Banbridge and District Historical Society, and Mrs Joan Logan Petticrew with the top of the old factory horn from Edenderry Factory, formerly occupied by Thomas Ferguson & Co. Ltd.

Brookfield Factory.

The Linen Industry

Banbridge from very early in its history was known as a linen town. The farmers grew the flax, scutched it at the water-powered mills and spun the yarns which were given out to hand-loom weavers who then wove the yarn into webs of cloth in their own cottages. The webs were collected by the farmer and then sold to the linen drapers at the Brown Linen Market (which used to stand where The Cut now is) before going to the bleach greens for bleaching, beetling and finishing. Many linen drapers took the finished webs of cloth all the way to Dublin on horseback with the webs strapped behind the saddle.

The growing trade in linen brought prosperity to Banbridge and consequently new and larger houses were erected. Town planning got under way in 1750, and suitable plots were laid out in the town to encourage building with leases being granted upon lives renewable forever. In 1756 a permit was granted for holding fairs and markets. The linen industry thrived with the coming of the industrial revolution, and the River Bann, which in Irish means 'white water', became renowned for its bleaching qualities with no less than 26 bleach greens in operation on the river between the townlands of Corbet and Moyallen by 1772. The industry was further boosted by the invention of power-loom weaving and spinning in the early 19th century, and it was at this time that great spinning mills such as Hayes at Seapatrick and Dunbar McMaster in the village of Gilford, the weaving factories of Smyth, Ferguson, McClelland and Wm. Walker in Banbridge and the bleach-works of Smyth, Cowdy, Nicholson, and Uprichard, all powered by the water of the River Bann, kept Banbridge at the forefront of world linen production. However, the development of man-made fibres and materials, easier to care for and less expensive, sounded the death knell for linen in the Banbridge area, and now just Thomas Ferguson and Co. (the only company in the world still producing double damask linen) exists in the area. It continues to supply the Royal Family with linen for the royal palaces. The name of Banbridge, however, will always remain famous for its history as the heart of a notable linen-producing area.

Brookfield Factory, former home of Smyth's Weaving Company.

Two

Sport

Mr Gilbert Beck on his motor-cycle in 1923. Gilbert was a participant in the old Bann hundred motor-cycle race held during the 1920s. This photograph was taken at the Spelga Pass in the Mourne mountains.

'The Dromara Destroyer' – Ray McCullough, who for years dominated the motorcycle road-racing scene winning his first race in 1960. He is a mechanical lab technician at Queens University, Belfast. Along with Professor Gordon Blair they designed and built their own QUB racing bikes. McCullough won a world championship grand prix in 1971 beating world champion Phil Reid. He went on to win three international grand prix races and three international North-West 200s. A rare visit to Oulton Park in England resulted in him beating rising star Barry Sheene.

Brian Reid. He comes from a sporting family just outside Banbridge and began his racing in 1976 at Aghadowey circuit on a 250 TD3 Yamaha. He soon became a consistent top-ten finisher and this pushed him into 'A' class at road races. Brian made his Isle of Man debut at the Manx Grand Prix in 1978 though he was forced to retire on this occasion and again in 1979. However, in 1980, riding a 500cc, he took second place. In 1980 he also rode at Tandragee, Cookstown, Killinchy and Dundrod. His career subsequently flourished with many race wins at the Isle of Man and other major road races at home in Ireland. Sad to say he was involved in a serious crash at the 'Temple' in 1994 which resulted in a badly broken leg and arm which forced him to retire after 18 years with a fantastic record of 5 TT wins, 10 Ulster Grand Prix wins, and 15 at the 'Temple' (second only to Ray McCullough's haul of 19). Perhaps the pinnacle of his career was winning the Formula Two World Championship in 1985 and 1986.

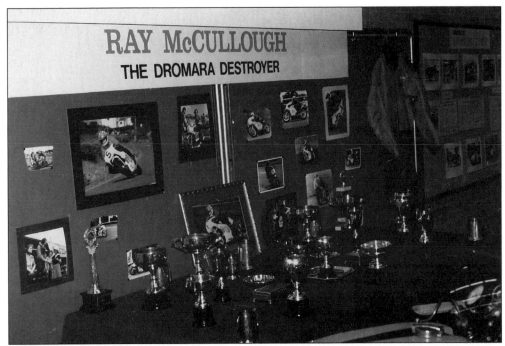

A display of trophies won by Ray McCullough plus photos and memorabilia on display at the Ulster Motor-Cycle Show.

Noel Hudson has been racing since he was nineteen. His first racing bike was a 750cc Triumph which he built himself with help from his mechanic Leslie Trimble. His first race was at Maghaberry in 1974, and his first win was in 1975 riding a 750 Kawasaki. His career continued through the '70s and '80s, but he had a major disappointment in 1985 after winning the 1000cc race at the Cookstown 100. His three bikes were taken to Portaferry along with those of Joey and Robert Dunlop to be loaded into a fishing boat for the trip to the Isle of Man for the TT. The boat unfortunately struck a rock and sank just outside Portaferry destroying all the machines, tools and leathers.

Denis McCullough, nephew of Ray McCullough, on his 125cc Honda at the 1996 Tandragee 100. Denis is following his Uncle Ray to the big time after winning the 125cc race at the 1997 Isle of Man TT.

John McCullough, another of Ray McCullough's nephews, on his 125cc Honda at the Killinchy 150 in 1995.

Nigel McCullough, yet another nephew of Ray McCullough, on his 125cc Honda at the Tandragee 100 in 1996.

Local jockey John Reid (right) who won the King George VI and Queen Elizabeth Stakes at Ascot in 1978 and 1997 and a host of other big races in the years between.

The Lilybank United football team in the 1920s.

A football match in Banbridge Football Club grounds, 1920s.

Banbridge Bosco FC pictured *c.* 1970. From left, back row: Jim Burns, Aidan Doyle, John McAleavey, Arthur Donaghy, Frank McCourt and Martin Campbell; middle row: Pat Meade, Ian Paxton, Kieran Smyth, Brian Jordan and Sean Doyle; front row: John Loy, Seamus Burns, Liam Porter, Terry Jordan and Malachy Wilson.

Down Shoes team members line up for the camera in 1972. From left, back row: G. Miskimmons (trainer), M. Miskimmons, G. Donaghy, S. McKay, S. Dowds, D. Craig, J. Willis, J. McCullough (manager); front row: G. Topping, C. Parkes, P. Willis, B. McCracken, J. Evans, P. Fearon.

This picture, taken in the 1970s, shows members of the Old Laurencetown Club of Halls Mill. Amongst those pictured are Jim Feeney (Irish champion and Irish international), his brother Alan, and Seamus Campbell and his brother Colin, from Banbridge.

Joe Little from Newry Street, a local boxer, pictured with one of his trophies in the early 1940s.

Banbridge Bowling Club, 1947. Amongst those pictured are, from left, back row: W. Gamble, J. Anderson, A. Martin, T. Arthur, W. McDermott, H. Brown, Horace Brown, H. McCaw; front row: Mr Jackson, W. Gracey, R. Mills, N. Cochrane, W. Chambers, S. McIlroy, J. Gault and T. Anderson.

Banbridge Angling Club once used the old mill ponds at Ballydown for hatching trout. From left, pictured c. 1950: K. Shooter, P. Downey, N. Carson, E. Jordan, -?-, J. McCourt, -?-.

Banbridge anglers pictured during the Star of the County Down Angling Competition, 1997. From left, front row: J. McRoberts, D. Clements, R. McClean; back row: E. Curran, S. Boyce, Cllr C. Vage (presenting award), R. Clements, W. Clingham.

Banbridge Hockey Club second XI pictured in the 1950s.

Banbridge hockey team, winners of the Kirk, Anderson and Keightly Senior cups, 1919-20 season. From left to right, back row: R. Simms, J. Morton, W. McMullan, F. McNeight, N. Coburn, J. McKeown; front row: J. Coburn, J.H. Harvey, T.N. Anderson (captain), H.C. Cull, F. McKee.

Banbridge hockey team, winners of the Anderson Cup, League and Kirk Cup finalists, 1920-21 season. From left to right, back row: J. Pepper, Joseph McKeown, J.H. Harvey, G. Farrel, J. Morton, R. Simms, H.C. Cull; front row: James McKeown, J. Coburn, T.N. Anderson (captain), N. Coburn and T. O'Connor.

Three
Railways

A railway line was constructed between Banbridge and Scarva in 1859. The linen industry was able to make use of this facility to bring coal for its steam engines and also to transport finished products. The Scarva line was one of the most scenic lines in Ireland passing many of the mills, and Drummiller and Drumaran lakes, as it followed the River Bann into Banbridge. In 1880 the line was extended to Ballyroney and ultimately on to Newcastle Co. Down, and, in 1863, a line was constructed from Banbridge to Belfast. The railway brought great prosperity to the town, but by 1957 all the various lines to and from Banbridge had closed. The only reminder of those busy days is the town's leisure centre which was converted from the railway station goods shed. The cuttings where the line once ran have become parkland and pleasant walks beside the beautiful River Bann.

Banbridge railway station, *c.* 1948, showing railcar 'A' in the Scarva Bay. On the up-platform is the multi-unit Railcar No 604, one of the 20 units built by AEC for the Great Northern Railway as substitutes for the steam-driven trains.

Railway foreman J. Dermott awaits the arrival of the Scarva branch train with U-class 197.440 and J19 coach replacing railcar 'A' at Banbridge railway station, 16 August 1952. The man standing beside the bicycle is Billy Stewart, a track-walker.

This is No 116.442T on the 5.22pm from Belfast coming into Banbridge station past the north signal-cabin, *c.* 1954.

Loco. No. 79.060 and train at Banbridge railway station shortly before closure, April 1956.

A wide view of Banbridge railway station with diesel train No 603 at the platform. This was the last train to leave the station in April 1956.

Loco. No. 101.060 taking water at Banbridge railway station with driver Jimmy Shields from Adelaide station. The crane in the background is there in preparation for lifting the tracks, c. 1959.

Four

Places

The little arch which ran from Railway Street onto Downshire Road. Illustration by C. McCaughey, 1995.

A view of The Cut from Bridge Street, 1920.

Weir's was in business in Banbridge in the early 20th century.

The Cut during the visit of Sir Edward Carson, 1913.

The Cut

It became evident in the early 19th century that the old road that had helped found Banbridge town was no longer adequate for the increasing amount of traffic through the town. A new road was constructed, therefore, and a wider, stronger bridge built over the River Bann in 1832 to replace the original rickety one. However, a new crisis was soon to follow, when the Postmaster General threatened to bypass the town if something was not done to alleviate the strain placed on the mail-coaches on the steep hill in Bridge Street. The town commissioners, realising this would be a disaster for the commercial life of the town, decided to make a cutting through the centre of the hill at a cost of £1,900. A grant of £500 was given by the principal landowner, the Marquis of Downshire, and so The Cut came into being thus changing the face of Bridge Street and paving the way for how it looks today. The old Market House which stood so proudly at the top of the hill had to be demolished to allow excavation of the cutting and a bridge was built over the cut to provide access to Scarva Street and Rathfriland Street. This bridge, Europe's first flyover, was built in 1834. Although solving the problem of the mail coaches, The Cut became an eyesore owing to the traders and townsfolk making it a receptacle for all the filth and refuse which they tipped into it every day. The situation became so bad that the town commissioners held a series of crisis meetings to see what could be done, and, at one such meeting, they very nearly decided to fill the whole thing in again. However, it was eventually decided to rebuild the walls with Mourne granite and make the cutting wider and deeper and erect a new wider bridge over the top. This was done with the aid of financial support from the Marquis of Downshire, the project being completed in 1885, and the new bridge with its four memorial lamps, one on each corner, was named Downshire Bridge in honour of the Marquis, a very benevolent landlord. This unique structure has become a famous landmark and has earned Banbridge the name of the town with the hole in the middle. The contractor was Mr Michael McCartan of Lisnaree outside Banbridge.

The Cut, still with the memorial lamps and drinking fountain, viewed from Newry Street in 1950.

Newry Street in the 1900s with a horse-drawn bread-cart in the foreground.

Newry Street in 1910 on a fair day.

Bridge Street in 1934 showing the Picture
House Café, Riddell's Home Bakery and the
Ulster Bank buildings. At the top of the tree is
townsman Hugh Anderson attempting to
rescue a cat.

The Brown Linen Market, from an illustration by William Hinks in 1783. This is probably the earliest-known illustration of Banbridge.

The Old Town Hall and Market House, *c*. 1980.

The new Civic Buildings which were opened in 1982 by Princess Alexandra.

The Central Bar was one of Banbridge's oldest public houses, retaining most of its original features up to its demolition in 1996. Mr Gerald McQuaid was the last owner until his death in 1995.

Gerald McQuaid, publican of the Central Bar, serving a drink to Sir Patrick Mayhew, Secretary of State for Northern Ireland, February 1993.

The Ulster Bar, established over one hundred years ago, was demolished in 1996. This public house was owned by the Bell family of Newry Street for over a hundred years and four generations.

Poplar Row, a small street behind the Ulster Bar, was home over the years to the Walsh, Feeney, Sheeghan, McKnight, Gartland, Major, Cunningham, Trainor, Clydesdale and Weir families. It was demolished in 1996, along with Bells, to make way for a new shopping complex.

Reilly Street in 1912.

Newry Road in 1921 showing the old turnpike house (front left of picture) and a horse-drawn bread-cart.

Church Street viewed from the River Bann in 1921.

Looking across the Bann from Church Street, 1957.

The Downshire Arms Hotel in Newry Street. Built in 1816 as an old coaching inn, the building has changed very little since then. Also pictured is the War Memorial.

The Stag's Head was owned by the McKee family for many years and is now an off-licence

The cobbled courtyard of the Downshire Arms Hotel, which has altered very little since the days when coaches such as the 'Fair Trader' ran between Belfast and Dublin.

Newry Street in the 1920s.

J. Coburn & Son,

Wholesale and Retail Seed Merchants,

IMPORTERS DUTCH AND RIGA FLAX SEEDS.

Agents Odam's Chemical Manure Co., the Ulster Manure Co.

P.S.—Feeding Stuffs of every kind always in stock.

NEWRY STREET,

BANBRIDGE.

Advertisement for Coburn's, 1904.

A view of Scarva Street as it was in the 1960s.

Reilly Street in the 1940s.

An illustration by Colin Turner of old houses at Huntly with Dunbars Bridge in the centre.

Mill-workers' cottages at Huntly in the 1960s.

Bridge Street in the 1920s.

Reavey's butcher's shop in 1933 with its Christmas display. From left: Bill Bryson, Patrick Reavey Snr, Patrick ('Peck') Reavey, Eddie Reavey and Andy Bryson.

Banbridge Courthouse which was built in 1873.

The Old Brewery - Banbridge

The Old Brewery, Castlewellan Road, which was built in 1840 as a brewery. After the death of the owner, however, it only survived for a few months, and, during the Famine in 1847, it was used to take the overspill from the workhouse. In 1853 it was converted to a bleach-works, and during the Second World War it was used as a military depot.

The Cut, viewed from Bridge Street in the 1970s.

The footbridge which linked Solitude House with Bridge Street, c. 1970. It was washed away in 1972 by floods.

DRAPERY.

Plain and Fancy
Dress Materials,
MANTLES & JACKETS,
Fur Capes
in all qualities.

MILLINERY.
Felt and Straw
Hats,
Ribbons,
Flowers,
Feathers,
Wings, &c.

LADIES',
GENTLEMEN'S,
AND
CHILDREN'S
Boots and Shoes
2,000 Pairs
to select from.

BLANKETS,
Cheapest & Best
in the Trade.

☞ Dress and
Mantle Making
done on the
premises. A perfect

L. MAIN,

General

Merchant,

47 & 49

Newry Street

BANBRIDGE.

Grocery
Department.
Family Groceries
TEAS A SPECIALTY
Provisions.

BUTTER
EXPORTER.

HARDWARE.
A large
assortment
of Lamps,
Brushes,
(Weavers'
Brushes),
Implements,
and Metal
Goods.

COALS.
Best Four-feet
Orrell.
Best Household
Coals.
Whitehaven
House Coals.
Cardiff and
Scotch Coals.

☞ Orders
promptly attended

Mrs L. Main was the proprietor of this establishment which was quite an emporium stocking everything from the proverbial anchor to a needle. This advertisement was taken from the *Household Almanac* for 1904.

Banbridge .

Bijou . . .

Minstrels. .

PROGRAMME.

Town Hall,

Thursday,

20th March, 1902.

"LET 'EM ALL COME."

To-Night at 8.

Dunbar McMaster and Co.'s mill at Gilford, 1976.

Dunbarton House, which was built for John Walsh McMaster, a partner in the Dunbar McMaster Company, in 1850.

Solitude House, home of the Clibborn
Family, who owned a flour-mill, a bleach
green and a factory in the immediate area.

FACTORY, BANBRIDGE, Co. DOWN

ROBINSON & CLEAVER'S Factory is at
Banbridge, Co. Down.

Here the finest linens in the world are
produced and distributed to our Stores in
Belfast. London, Liverpool and Bournemouth.

When you are in N. Ireland we cordially
invite you to visit our Belfast Store (opposite
City Hall), and inspect the extensive range
of Household Linens, Handkerchiefs, etc.

ROBINSON & CLEAVER LTD.
BELFAST   ::   **N. IRELAND**

This is an advertisement for Robinson and
Cleaver Ltd, whose factory was situated on
Castlewellan Road. They were linen
manufacturers until their closure in the 1960s.

95

Downshire or Jinglers Bridge with the McClelland Memorial Fountain to the right-hand side. The nickname 'Jinglers' derives from an apple seller who used to have a stall there. She jingled the coins in her pocket as she paced up and down selling her wares.

The McClelland Memorial Fountain in the grounds of the Civic Buildings. This fountain used to stand on the Jinglers Bridge but had to be moved owing to the volume of traffic using the bridge in modern times.

The memorial on Downshire Road to Joseph Scriven, the author of the hymn, *What a friend we have in Jesus*.

The Anglers Rest public house at Corbet on the road between Banbridge and Newcastle.

Church Square, showing the Crozier Memorial in the foreground, with Seapatrick parish church in the trees, and next to it, Banbridge Masonic Hall, 1936.

Avonmore House, birthplace of Captain Francis Rawdon Moira Crozier, which was built in 1791.

Captain Crozier

Captain F.R.M. Crozier RN was born on the 17 September 1796 at Avonmore House in Church Square, Banbridge. He was the tenth child (of twelve) of George Crozier, a Banbridge solicitor. In 1810, aged 14, Francis joined the Navy at Cork and underwent training as an officer. He passed his mate's exams in February 1817 and served at the Cape of Good Hope until his return to England in 1821. Later that same year he sailed as mate on HMS *Fury* with Captain William Parry, later to become Admiral Sir William Parry RN, in search of the North West Passage. In 1824 and 1827, he also went with Parry in search of the exact location of the North Pole. During these years of exploration, young Crozier formed a lifelong friendship with James Clark Ross who had been mate on HMS *Heckla* in 1821 and on the other polar voyages.

In 1843 Crozier heard that the Admiralty was organising another expedition in search of the North West Passage. This time Sir John Franklin was chosen as leader with Crozier as second in command. The expedition set sail on 19 May 1845 and spent its first winter stuck fast on the ice at Beechey Island, but despite this only three men died during that first winter. The name of the expedition's two ships were HMS *Terror* and HMS *Erebus*, and during the second winter they were again trapped in the ice. In 1847 the expected summer thaw did not set in so the ships had to remain stationary. In June, Sir John Franklin died and Crozier took command with James Fitzjames as second in command. By the spring of 1848, nine officers and fifteen crew were dead, so Crozier decided to load the sledges with provisions and lead the crew southwards on foot over the ice to the mainland. One by one they slowly perished along the way presumably from scurvy and starvation. Search parties were sent by the Admiralty to ascertain the fate of the expedition, but it was not until the autumn of 1851 that their first winter camp was discovered.

More information was gathered in April 1854 by John Rae, an Orkney Islander employed as a surgeon by the Hudson Bay Company, when an Inuit man told him of a group of white men who died near the mouth of the river. The Inuit people gave him some souvenirs including a spoon and fork which bore the Crozier family crest. Lady Franklin, widow of Sir John, financed another expedition under the leadership of Leopold McClintock, an Ulsterman. His second-in-command found a cairn which contained a single sheet of paper bearing two messages. The first, dated 28 May 1847, gave their position in the ice, while the second, dated 25 April 1848, read, 'H.M. Ships 'Terror' and 'Erebus' were deserted on April 22, 5 leagues N.N.W. of this point', then in Crozier's hand, 'We start tomorrow for Beck's Fish River.' So ended the career of a most noble officer and heroic son of the Bann.

In 1862, a most impressive memorial was erected to his memory in 1862 opposite his birthplace, that fine old Georgian house built by his father in 1791. A memorial plaque was also erected in Holy Trinity, Seapatrick parish church, the church in which he was baptised and where he and his family worshipped. The plaque depicts the two ships *Terror* and *Erebus* marooned in the ice. Both the monument and his birthplace stand proudly in Church Square to this day reminding us of Banbridge's most famous son.

Drumballyroney Church and School where Patrick Brontë preached and taught.

The Brontë Connection

In a white-washed cottage at Emdale outside Banbridge on St Patrick's Day, 17 March 1777, a son was born to Hugh and Eleanor Brunty. The child, their first-born, was christened Patrick.

Patrick grew up to be a strong young man with dark red hair and pale blue eyes. He taught himself to read and write from the three or four books his illiterate parents chanced to own. He was apprenticed to a blacksmith but later worked as a linen weaver and later still worked for a draper. By the time he was 16, Patrick was teaching in the Presbyterian school at Glascar and later in the Drumballyroney Parish Church School. The Vicar of Drumgooland, Rev Thomas Tighe invited him to teach his two young sons. Rev Tighe was a friend of John Wesley, leader of the Methodist Society, who stayed with him on his preaching tours in Ireland. Rev Tighe coached Patrick, lent him a little money, and sponsored him to St John's College, Cambridge, which Patrick entered in 1802 at the age of 25.

Patrick took his degree in 1806, was ordained and then held curacies in Essex and Shropshire before finally coming to Yorkshire in 1809, having been recommended to a vicar there by William Morgan a fellow curate, who, like Patrick, had Wesleyan friends. While staying at Bradford, Patrick was introduced to Miss Marca Bramwell, a well-educated young lady whom he subsequently fell in love with and married in December 1812.

Six children were born of the Brontë marriage, Marca in 1813, Elizabeth in 1815, Charlotte in 1816, Patrick Bramwell in 1817, Emily in 1818, and Anne in 1820.

In 1820 Patrick was appointed incumbent of Haworth, but unfortunately his wife died of cancer in 1821, and from then on Haworth became the permanent Brontë home. Here, on the bleak Yorkshire Moors Charlotte, Emily and Anne found the inspiration for their books. So from humble beginnings in County Down came a literary family which became famous all over the world for books such as *Wuthering Heights, Jane Eyre* and *The Tenant of Wildfell Hall.*

Five
Places of Worship

Glascar Presbyterian Church, 1980.

Left: Magherally parish church. *Right*: Helen Waddell's grave at Magherally parish church. She was a scholar of medieval history and translated many ancient Celtic and Chinese writings into English. She was also an internationally renowned author and spent much time staying with relatives at Magherally, a place she loved and where she requested to be buried.

The old façade of Scarva Street Presbyterian Church, 1956.

An aerial view of Seapatrick parish church in the 1940s.

The interior of Scarva Street Presbyterian Church in 1897.

Aghaderg Parish Church Hall, formerly the Glebe School, 1981.

Loughbrickland Presbyterian Church and graveyard, 1990.

Six
Events

Military procession in Bridge Street in the early 1900s, possibly to mark the end of the Boer War.

A crowd gathering in Church Street at the turn of the century for a temperance march associated with the catch-me-pal movement.

These two pictures of Bridge Street were taken during the Silver Jubilee of King George V and Queen Mary in 1935.

Rathfriland Street decorated for the coronation of King George VI and Queen Elizabeth in 1937.

A 1924 'Bullnose' Morris Cowley at Waringstown Vintage Cavalcade, 1997. From left: Pat Lavery, Aubrey Patterson and John Scott.

Mr and Mrs George Cairns with their vintage Singer Gazelle. Both this and the below picture were taken at the 1997 Waringstown Vintage Cavalcade.

Mervyn Allen and Ivor Erwin with their vintage motorcycles.

Walking-stick expert, Eddie Carr, demonstrates his craft to visitor Libby McCalla at an exhibition in the Old Town Hall, 1997.

Residents and staff from Crozier House, Banbridge who won a number of baking and craft awards at the 1997 Lurgan Show. From left, front row: Maggie Downey, Violet Blakely and Emily Russell; back row: Suzannah Fleming, May Macavoy (care assistant and craft co-ordinator), Margaret McAuley (manager), Harriet Lyttle and Maura Hylands.

Pictured at the Special Service and Presentation in Banbridge Baptist Church to mark the retirement, after seventeen years, of Pastor S.T. and Mrs Christine Carson. From left, front row: Miss Evelyn Watson, Mrs Carson, Pastor Carson and Matthew Adams (treasurer); back row: Winston Annett (secretary), Pastor Wesley Crawford, David McCrum and Dickson McCrum (elders).

Part of an exhibition at Scarva Visitors Centre in 1995.

Former Banbridge man Mike Shields, now living in Boston, recently enjoyed a visit back to the town, where he played a round of golf with old friends, July 1997. From left: Tom Fee, Benny McConville, Gene Fitzpatrick and Mike Shields.

Banbridge St Vincent De Paul Society taking possession of their new van from the Banbridge District Partnership. Vincent Sands, vice-president, accepts the keys from Margaret Thompson and Margaret Campbell, joint chairpersons of Banbridge District Partnership, July 1997.

Members of Banbridge Choral Society who presented their musical *Clown* at the Waterford Festival, summer 1997.

Members of the Banbridge Campus UBIFHE Historical Group at the announcement of their plans to commemorate the Great Famine, November 1996. From left, front row: Dr Audrey McKeown (Campus manager), Frank Downey (group lecturer) and Angela Dillon (secretary of Historical Group); back row: Mary Jeffers, Tom Moore and Helen Adams.

Banbridge Archery Club members Alan Convery, David Holt and Cathy Davison, July 1997.

Sports award winners at the St Mary's Primary School annual prize distribution, July 1997.

Edenderry pupils with the awards they picked up at the end-of-year assembly, July 1997.

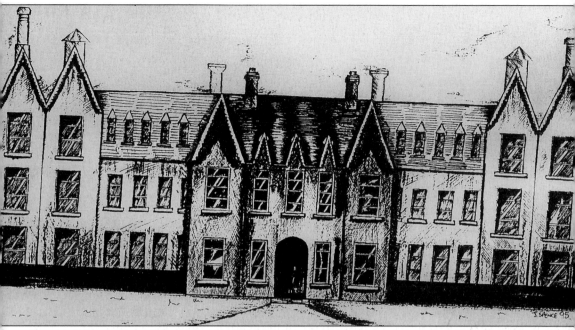

An artist's impression of the Banbridge Workhouse.

The Workhouse

In 1841 a workhouse was built in Banbridge by the Banbridge Poor Law Union for the relief of the poor of the district. When the Great Famine spread through Ireland in 1845, after blight destroyed the potato crop, Banbridge did not escape the suffering that it brought. By 1846 numbers in the workhouse had risen to 500, disease was rampant, and, during the winter of 1846-47, snow covered the whole country thus greatly adding to the distress. Deaths averaged 14 per week and overcrowding caused many people to be turned away at the gates. By 1848 the workhouse numbers began decreasing, and things began to improve with prosperity returning once more to Banbridge. The workhouse continued to function until 1932 when it was closed and was redeveloped into a hospital. Unfortunately, changes in the delivery of health services, meant that the hospital was closed at the end of 1996, leaving the townsfolk of Banbridge with a journey to Newry or Craigavon for hospital treatment.

Banbridge Workhouse under conversion into Banbridge Hospital in the 1930s.

Banbridge Silver Band playing at the local hospital for the last time on Christmas Day 1996, bringing to an end a traditional engagement of over sixty years.

A Banbridge orchestra at the turn of the century.

Banbridge Conservative Flute Band in 1914.

Banbridge Brass Band in August 1924.

Geoghegan Memorial Pipe Band from Loughbrickland in the 1970s.

Geoghegan Memorial Pipe Band with their trophies in 1993. They were world champions 1992/93. From left, back row: D/M Norman Nicholl, Ian Copeland, John Geoghegan, Steven Nicholl, Moira Cully, Uel Weir, Neil Anderson, Trevor Hylands, Graham Wilson, P/M Trevor Weir, David Cairns, D/S S. Smyth, P/S N. Beck, Jason Cannaway, Nigel Anderson, Jim Ervine, Alison Bell, Judith Bell, Philip Bell, Tom Bell, Adrian Fairley. Two members of the band – Andrew Bryson and Paul Beck – were absent when this photograph was taken.

Cavan Pipe Band, Rathfriland in the 1960s.

Belmont, a former linen-house, now a well-known local hotel, 1993.

Constable William Keenan, Royal Ulster Constabulary, outside Mr William Bambrick's saddler's shop in Newry Street in the 1920s.

Acknowledgements

We would like to thank all those who lent photographs for inclusion in this book, amongst whom were: Banbridge and District Historical Society, Banbridge Heritage Development Limited, Mr George Armstrong, Miss E. Beck, Mr Bobby Brown, Mr J.R. Dillon, Mrs Annabel Douglas and Mr Dennis McAleenan.

We would also like to thank the photographers, many of whom are anonymous, who took time to record the passing scenes in Banbridge. Last, but by no means least, thanks must also go to Mr Philip Magennis, Mr Bruce White and the staff of Banbridge Heritage Development Limited for their help in sorting the photographs, writing captions and constructing the layout.